RAIL-ROAD USURPATION OF NEW JERSEY.

SPEECH

OF

HON. CHARLES SUMNER,

OF MASSACHUSETTS,

ON THE ACT TO REGULATE COMMERCE AMONG THE SEVERAL STATES.

IN THE SENATE OF THE UNITED STATES, FEBRUARY 14TH, 1865.

NEW YORK YOUNG MEN'S REPUBLICAN UNION:
1865.

NEW YORK YOUNG MEN'S REPUBLICAN UNION

1856–1860–1864.

OFFICERS.

MARK HOYT, *President.*
DEXTER A. HAWKINS, *Vice-President*
FRANK W. BALLARD, *Corresponding Secretary.*
CHARLES T. RODGERS, *Treasurer.*

BOARD OF CONTROL.

CEPHAS BRAINERD, *Chairman.*
MARK HOYT.
DEXTER A. HAWKINS.
FRANK W BALLARD.
CHARLES T. RODGERS.
BENJAMIN F. MANIERRE.
THOMAS L. THORNELL.
WILLIAM M. FRANKLIN.
CHARLES C. NOTT.
GEORGE H. MATHEWS.

RAIL-ROAD USURPATION OF NEW JERSEY.

SPEECH

OF

HON. CHARLES SUMNER,

OF MASSACHUSETTS,

ON THE ACT TO REGULATE COMMERCE AMONG THE SEVERAL STATES.

In the Senate of the United States, February 14, 1865.

The proposition under consideration was in the following terms:

"AN ACT TO REGULATE COMMERCE AMONG THE SEVERAL STATES.

"*Be it enacted by the Senate and House of Representatives of the United States of America in Congress assembled*, That every railroad company in the United States whose road is operated by steam, its successors and assigns, be, and is hereby, authorized to carry upon and over its road, connexions, boats, bridges, and ferries, all freight, property, mails, passengers, troops, and government supplies on their way from any State to another State, and to receive compensation therefor."

Mr. President, the question before us concerns the public convenience to a remarkable degree. But it concerns also the unity of this Republic. Look at it in its simplest form, and you will confess its importance. Look at it in its political aspect, and you will recognize how vital it is to the integrity of the Union itself. On one side we encounter a formidable Usurpation with all the pretensions of State rights, hardly less flagrant and pernicious than those which have ripened in bloody rebellion. On the other side are the simple and legitimate claims of the Union under the Constitution of the United States.

Thus stands the question at the outset. Public convenience and the Union itself in its beneficent powers on the one side. Public inconvenience and all the discord of intolerable State pretensions on the other side.

The proposition on its face is applicable to all the States throughout the Union, and in its *vital principle* it concerns every lover of his country. But it cannot be disguised that the interest which it has excited in the other House, and also in the Senate, must be referred to its bearing on the railroads of New Jersey. Out of this circumstance springs the ardor of opposition; perhaps, also, something of the ardor of support. Therefore pardon me if I glance one moment at the geographical position of this State, and its railroad Usurpation in the name of State rights.

Look on the map, or better still, consult your own personal experience in the journey from Washington to New York, and you will find that New Jersey lies on the great line of travel between the two capitals of the country, political and commercial. There it is, directly in the path. It cannot be avoided except by a circuitous journey. On this single line commerce, passengers, mails, troops—all must move. In the chain of communication by which capital is bound to capital—nay more, by which the Union itself is bound together, there is no single link of equal importance. Strike it out, and where are you? Your capitals will be separated and the Union itself will be loosened. But the evil sure to follow, if this link were struck out, must follow also in proportionate extent from every interference with that perfect freedom of transit through New Jersey which I now ask in behalf of commerce, passengers, mails and troops.

Such is the geographical position of New Jersey. And it is here on this highway of travel that pernicious pretensions have been set up which can be overthrown only by the power of Congress. The case is plain.

New Jersey, in the exercise of pretended State rights, has undertaken to invest the Camden and Amboy Railroad Company with unprecedented prerogatives. These are the words of the Legislature: "It shall not be lawful, at any time during the said railroad charter, to construct any other railroads in this State without the consent of the said companies, which shall be intended or used for the transportation of passengers or merchandise *between the cities of New York and Philadelphia*, or to compete in business with the railroad authorized by the act to which this supplement is relative." (New Jersey Session Laws for 1854, page 387.) Here, in barefaced terms, is the grant of a monopoly in all railroad transportation, whether of commerce, passengers, mails, or troops, between *New York*, a city *outside* of New Jersey, and *Philadelphia*, another city *outside* of New Jersey. Or, looking at this grant of monopoly again, we shall find that *while it leaves the local transportation of New Jersey untouched*, it undertakes to regulate and appropriate the transportation between two great cities outside of New Jersey, constituting, from geographical position, the gates through which the whole mighty movement, north and south, must pass.

If this monopoly is offensive on its face, it becomes still more offensive when we consider the motive in which it had its origin. By the confession of its supporters, it was granted in order to raise a revenue for the State out of men and business not of the State. It was an ingenious device to tax commerce, passengers, mails, and troops in their transit across New Jersey, from State to State. Here is a confession, which will be found in the legislative journal of New Jersey, as long ago as 1841, in a document from the executive committee of the coalesced railroads, represented by the Camden and Amboy Company:

"It seems plain, from the acts incorporating these companies, and the testimony of those best conversant with the history of their incorporations, that it was the policy of the State, *taking advantage of the geographical position of New Jersey*, between the largest States and cities of the Union *to create a revenue by imposing tax or transit duty upon every person who should pass on the railroad across the State* between those cities from the Delaware river to the Raritan bay; but that it was not their design to impose any tax upon citizens of their own State for traveling between intermediate places." * * * * "Here, again, the policy and intention of the State is most clearly indicated in exempting her own citizens from the operation of this system of taxation."—Page 29.

And here are the words of another functionary equally frank, belonging to the same railroad connection:

"The Company believe that a careful consideration of the whole matter, as well from the provisions of the charter as from a recurrence to the period when it was granted, will produce the conviction that *the transit duty was intended to be levied only on citizens of other States passing through New Jersey.*"

The spirit in which this tax has been laid will appear from another incident which cannot be without interest to the Senators from New York. The Erie railroad, which is so important to transportation in the great State which they represent on this floor, has been compelled, in addition to the usual tax on that part of the road in New Jersey, to pay an extra tax in the shape of "a transit duty of three cents on every passenger and two cents on every ton of goods, wares, and merchandise, *except passengers and freight transported exclusively within* this State." This imposition was as late as 1862, and it is a part of that same system which constitutes the railroad Usurpation of New Jersey.

But the character of this Usurpation becomes still more apparent in the conduct adopted toward another railroad in New Jersey. It appears that a succession of railroads has been constructed, under charters of this State, from Raritan Bay, opposite New York, to Camden, opposite Philadelphia, constituting a continuous line, suitable for transportation, across New Jersey and between the two great cities of New York and Philadelphia. The continuous line is known as the Raritan and Delaware Bay Railroad. On the breaking out of the rebellion, when Washington was menaced by a wicked enemy, and the patriots of the land were aroused to sudden efforts, the Quartermaster-General of the United States directed the transportation of troops, horses, baggage, and munitions of war, from New York to Philadelphia over this line. The other railroad, claiming a monopoly, filed a bill in equity, praying that the Raritan and Delaware Bay Railroad "be decreed to desist and refrain" from such transportation, and also praying "that an *account* may be taken to ascertain the amount of damages." The counsel of the monopoly openly insisted that, by this transportation, the State was "robbed of her ten cents a passenger;" and then cried out, "I say it is no defense whatever if they have succeeded in obtaining an order of the Secretary of War, *when we call upon them to give us the money they made by it;* and that is one of our calls. They have no right to get an order to deprive the State of New Jersey of the right of transit duty, *which is her adopted policy.*" Such was the argument of Mr. Stockton, counsel for the monopoly, November 12, 1863. The *transit duty* is vindicated as the *adopted policy* of New Jersey. Surely, in the face of such pretensions, it was time that something should be done by Congress.

Such, sir, are the pretensions of New Jersey to interfere with commerce, passengers, mails, and troops *from other States*, on their way, it may be, to the national capital, even with necessary succors at a moment of national peril. Such pretensions, persistently maintained and vindicated, constitute a Usurpation not only hostile to the public interests, but menacing to the Union itself. Here is no question of local taxation, or local immunities, under State laws; but an open assumption by a State to tax the commerce of the United States on its way from State to State.

From the nature of the case, and according to every rule of reason, there ought to be a remedy for such a grievance. No usurping monopoly ought to be allowed to establish itself in any State across the national highway, and, like a baron of the middle ages perched in his rocky fastness, levy tolls and tribute from all the wayfarers of business, pleasure, or duty. The nuisance should be abated. The Usurpation should be overthrown. And happily the powers are ample under the Constitution of the United States. Following unquestionable principles and authentic precedents, the committee have proposed a remedy which I now proceed to discuss.

The bill under consideration was originally introduced by me into the Senate. It was afterward adopted and passed by the other House as a substitute for a kindred bill which was pending there. Beyond the general interest which I take in the public business, this is my special reason for entering into this discussion.

The bill is arraigned as unconstitutional. But this objection is a common-place of opposition. When all other reasons fail, then is the Constitution invoked. Such an attempt on such an occasion attests to my mind the weakness of the cause. It is little better than the assertion of an *alias* in a criminal case.

The entire and unimpeachable constitutionality of the present measure is apparent in certain familiar precepts of the Constitution, which were brought to view in the title and preamble of the bill as introduced by me, but which have been omitted in the bill now bofore us. The title of the bill as introduced by me was, "to facilitate commercial, postal, and military communication among the several States." This title opens the whole constitutional question. This was followed by a preamble, as follows:

> "Whereas the Constitution of the United States confers upon Congress, in express terms, the power to regulate commerce among the several States, to establish post roads, and to raise and support armies: Therefore, *Be it enacted.*"

In these few words three sources of power are clearly indicated, either of which is ample; but the three together constitute an overrunning fountain.

First. There is the power "to regulate commerce among the several States." Look at the Constitution and you will find these identical words. From the great sensitiveness of States this power has been always exercised by Congress with peculiar caution; but it still lives to be employed by an enfranchised Government.

In asserting this power I follow not only the text of the Constitution, but also the authoritative decisions of the Supreme Court of the United States. Perhaps there is no question in our constitutional history which has been more clearly illustrated by our greatest authority, Chief Justice Marshall. In the well known case where the State of New York had undertaken to grant an exclusive right to navigate the waters of New York by vessels propelled by steam, the illustrious Chief Justice, speaking for the court, declared the restriction to be illegal, because it interfered with commerce between the States precisely as is now done by New Jersey. In his opinion commerce was something more than traffic or the transportation of property. It was also "the commercial intercourse between nations and parts of nations in all its branches," and it embraced by necessary inference *all inter-State communications* and the whole subject of intercourse between the people of the several States. It was declared that the power of Congress over the subject was not limited by State lines, but that it was co-extensive with commerce itself, according to the enlarged signification of the term. Here are the words of Chief Justice Marshall:

"But in regulating commerce with foreign nations, the power of Congress does not stop at the jurisdictional lines of the several States. It would be a very useless power if it could not pass these lines. Every district has a right to participate in it. The deep streams which penetrate our country in every direction pass through the interior of almost every State in the Union, and furnish the means for exercising this right. *If Congress has the power to regulate it, that power must be exercised wherever the subject exists.* If it exists within the States, if a foreign voyage may commence or terminate at a port within a State, then the power of Congress may be exercised within a State."—*Gibbons* vs. *Ogden*, 9 *Wheaton*, 196.

This important decision of the Supreme Court was before railroads. It grew out of an attempt to appropriate certain navigable thoroughfares of the Union. But it is equally applicable to those other thoroughfares of the Union, where the railroad is the substitute for water. It is according to the genius of jurisprudence, that a rule once established governs all cases which come within the original reason on which it was founded. Therefore I conclude confidently that the power of Congress over internal commerce by railroad is identical with that over internal commerce by water. But this decision does not stand alone.

Mr. Justice Story, who was a member of the Supreme Court at this time, in a later decision thus explains the extent of this power:

"It does not stop at the mere boundary line of a State; nor is it confined to acts done on the water, or in the necessary course of the navigation thereof. *It extends to such acts done on land as interfere with*, obstruct, or prevent *the free exercise of the power to regulate commerce* with foreign nations and *among the States*."—*United States* vs. *Coombs*, 12 *Peters*, 78.

From various cases illustrating this power I call attention to that known as the Passenger case, where the Supreme Court declared that the statutes of New York and Massachusetts, imposing taxes upon alien passengers arriving at the ports of those States, was in derogation of the Constitution. On this occasion Mr. Justice McLean said:

"Shall passengers, admitted by act of Congress without a tax, be taxed by a State? The supposition of such a power in a State is utterly inconsistent with a commercial power, either paramount or exclusive in Congress."

Mr. Justice Grier said, with great point:

"To what purpose commit to Congress the power of regulating our intercourse with foreign nations and among the States, *if these regulations may be changed at the discretion of each State?*" * * * * "It is, therefore, not left to the discretion of each State of the Union either to refuse a right of passage to persons or property, or to exact a duty on permission to exercise it."—7 *Howard*, 464.

But this is the very thing that is now done by New Jersey, which "exacts a duty" from passengers across the State.

Mr. JOHNSON. Do I understand the Senator to be quoting from the Passenger case?

Mr. SUMNER. Yes, sir.

Mr. JOHNSON. That was a case where the legislation of Massachusetts was brought before the court.

Mr. SUMNER. I have already stated that there were two State offenders at that time; there is now only one.

I call attention also to the case of the Wheeling bridge, where Congress, under peculiar circumstances, exercised this identical power. In this case the State of Pennsylvania claimed the power to limit and control the transit across the Ohio river to the State of Ohio, and this power was affirmed by the Supreme Court so long as Congress refrained from legislation on the subject. But under the pressure of a public demand, and in the exercise of the very powers which are now invoked, Congress has declared the Wheeling bridge to be a lawful structure, anything in any State law to the contrary notwithstanding. The Supreme Court, after the passage of this act, denied a motion to punish the owners of the bridge for a contempt in rebuilding it, and affirmed that the act declaring the Wheeling bridge a lawful structure was within the legitimate exercise by Congress of its constitutional power to regulate commerce. (13 Howard, 528.) But it is this very power which is here invoked in a case more important, and far more urgent, than that of the Wheeling bridge.

There is also another case where Congress has exercised this power precisely as is now proposed. I refer to the Steubenville bridge and Holliday's Cove railroad across the Ohio, in what is called the Panhandle of Virginia. This bridge was first attempted under a charter granted by Virginia, but Congress at last interfered and enacted :

"That the bridge partly constructed across the Ohio river at Steubenville, in the State of Ohio, abutting on the Virginia shore of said river, is hereby declared to be *a lawful structure.*

"That the said bridge and Holliday's Cove railroad are hereby declared a public highway, and established a *post road* for the purpose of transmission of mails of the United States."—12 *Statutes at Large*, 569.

Such are the precedents of courts and of statutes showing how completely this power belongs to Congress in the regulation of internal commerce. The authorities are plain and explicit. They cannot be denied. They cannot be explained away. It would be superfluous to dwell on them. There they stand like so many granite columns, fit supports of that internal commerce which in itself is a chief support of the Union.

Secondly. There is also the power "to establish post roads," which is equally explicit. Here, too, the words are plain, and they have received an authoritative exposition. It is with reference to these words that Mr. Justice Story remarks that "constitutions of government do not turn upon ingenious subtleties, but are adapted to the business and exigencies of human society; and the powers given are understood, in a large sense, in order to secure the public interests. Common sense becomes the guide, and prevents men from dealing with mere logical abstractions." (Story, Commentaries on Constitution, vol. 2, sec. 1134.) The same learned authority, in considering these words of the Constitution, seems to have anticipated the very question now under consideration. Here is a passage which may fitly close the argument on this head :

"Let a case be taken *when State policy*"—

As, for instance, in New Jersey at this time—

"or State hostility shall lead the Legislature to close up or discontinue a road, the nearest and the best between two great States, rivals, perhaps, for the trade and intercourse of a third State; shall it be said that Congress has no right to make or repair a road for keeping open for the mail the best means of communication between those States? May the national Government be compelled to take the most inconvenient and indirect routes for the mail? *In other words, have the States the power to say how, and upon what roads, the mails shall and shall not travel?* If so, then, in relation to post roads, the States, and not the Union, are supreme."—*Story, Commentaries on the Constitution,* vol. 2, sec. 1144.

Thirdly. Then comes the power "to raise and support armies:" an unquestionable power lodged in Congress. But this grant carries with it, of course, all incidental powers necessary to the execution of the principal power. It would be absurd to suppose that Congress could raise an army, but could not authorize the agencies required for its transportation from place to place. Congress has not been guilty of any such absurdity. Already it has by formal act proceeded "to authorize the President of the United States in certain cases to take possession of railroads and telegraphs, and for other purposes." (12 Statutes at Large, p. 334.) By this act the President is empowered "to take possession of any or all the railroad lines in the United States, their rolling stock, their offices, shops, buildings, and all their appendages and appurtenances," and it is declared that any such railroad "shall be considered as a post road and a part of the military establishment of the United States." Here is the exercise of a broader power than any which is now proposed. The less must be contained in the greater.

Mr. President, such are the three sources of power in the Constitution, each and all applicable to the present case. Each is indisputable. Therefore the conclusion, which is sustained by each, is three times indisputable.

So plain is this power that it has been admitted by New Jersey in a legislative act, as follows :

"SEC. 6. *Be it enacted,* That when any other railroad or roads for the transportation of passengers and property between New York and Philadelphia across this State shall be constructed and used for that purpose, under or by virtue of *any law of this State or the United States authorizing or recognizing said road,* that then and in that case the said dividends shall be no longer payable to the State, and the said stock shall be re-transferred to the Company by the treasurer of this State."

Thus, in formal words, has New Jersey actually anticipated the very measure now under consideration. All that is now proposed so far as New Jersey is concerned is simply *to recognize other railroads for the transportation of passengers and property between New York and Philadelphia across this State.*

Such is the argument in brief for the constitutionality of the present bill, whether it be regarded as a general measure applicable to all the railroads of the country, or only applicable to the railroads of New Jersey. The case is so plain and absolutely unassailable that I should leave it on this simple exhibition if the Senator from Maryland, [Mr. JOHNSON,] who always brings to these questions the authority of professional reputation, had not most zealously argued the other way. According to him the bill is unconstitutional. Let me say, however, that the conclusion of the learned Senator is only slightly sustained by the reasons which he assigns. Indeed his whole elaborate argument, if brought to the touchstone, will be found inconclusive and unsatisfactory.

The Senator opened with the proposition that the internal commerce of a State is within the exclusive jurisdiction of the State, and from this he argued that the present bill is unconstitutional. But the Senator will allow me to say that his proposition is not sufficiently broad for his conclusion. The present bill does not touch the internal commerce of a State, except so far as it may be a link in the chain of "commerce among States," which is committed by the Constitution to the jurisdiction of Congress. Mark this distinction, I pray you: for it is essential to a right understanding of the case.

From this inapplicable proposition the Senator passed to another equally inapplicable. He asserted that the jurisdiction of a State over all territory within the limits was exclusive, so that the United States cannot obtain jurisdiction over any portion thereof, except by assent of the State; and from this again he argued the unconstitutionality of the present bill. But this very illustration seems to have been anticipated by Mr. Justice Story in his learned Commentaries, where he shows conclusively, first, that it is inapplicable, and secondly, that so far as it is applicable, it is favorable to the power. Here are his words:

"The clause respecting cessions of territory for the seat of Government, and for forts, arsenals, dock-yards, &c., has nothing to do with the point. *But if it had, it is favorable to the power.*" * * * * * *

"But surely it will not be pretended that Congress could not erect a fort or magazine in a place within a State unless the State should cede the territory. The only effect would be that the jurisdiction in such a case would not be exclusive. Suppose a State should prohibit a sale of any of the lands within its boundaries by its own citizens, for any public purposes indispensable for the Union, either military or civil, would not Congress possess a constitutional right to demand and appropriate land within the State for such purposes, making a just compensation? *Exclusive jurisdiction over a road is one thing; the right to make it is another.* A turnpike company may be authorized to make a road, and yet may have no jurisdiction, or at least no exclusive jurisdiction, over it."—2 *Story on Constitution.* sec. 1146.

Had the distinguished commentator anticipated the argument of the Senator from Maryland, he could not have answered it more completely.

Passing from these constitutional generalities the Senator came at once to an assumption, which, if it were sustained, would limit essentially the power of Congress with regard to post roads. According to him the words of the Constitution authorizing Congress "to establish post roads," means only that it shall designate roads already existing; and in support of this assumption he relied upon the message of Mr. Monroe in 1822, on the Cumberland road. The learned Senator adds that this is "the received opinion uniformly acted upon and since recognized as the correct opinion by the judiciary." Of course his testimony on this point is important; but it is overruled at once by the authority I have already cited, which says that "the power to establish post offices and post roads has never been understood to include no more than the power to *point out* and *designate* post offices and post roads." (Story's Commentaries, vol. 2, sec. 1136.) In the face of Mr. Justice Story's dissent, expressed in his authoritative Commentaries, it is impossible to say that it is "the received opinion," as has been asserted by the Senator. But the learned commentator insists that "the Constitution itself uniformly uses the word *establish* in the general sense and never in this peculiar and narrow sense," and after enumerating various places where it occurs, says, "it is plain that to construe the word in any of these cases as equivalent to *designate* or *point out* would be absolutely absurd. The clear import of the word is to create and form and fix in a settled manner." "To establish post offices and post roads is to frame and pass laws, to erect, make, form, regulate, and preserve them. Whatever is necessary, whatever is appropriate to this purpose, is within the power." (*Ibid.*, sec. 1131.) I might quote other words from the same authority; but this is enough to vindicate the power which the Senator has denied.

But here it is my duty to remind the Senate that the argument of the Senator from Maryland on this head is not only false in its assumption, but that the assumption, even if correct, is entirely inapplicable on the present occasion. The bill now before the Senate does not undertake to create, but simply to *designate or point out*, certain roads. Therefore it does not fall under the objection which the Senator has adduced. Even by his own admission it is constitutional.

But the Senator, not content with an erroneous assumption concerning post roads, which, even if correct, is entirely inapplicable, made another assumption concerning another clause of the Constitution which was equally erroneous and inapplicable. The Senator argued that the railroad charters in New Jersey were grants in the nature of a contract, and that they were protected by "the constitutional inhibition upon States interfering with contracts;" and here he referred to several decisions of the Supreme Court of the United States. I do not trouble you with the decisions. It will be enough if I call attention to the precise text of the Constitution, which is: "*No State* shall pass any law impairing the obligation of contracts."

Look at these words, and it appears, in the first place, that this prohibition is addressed to the States and not to Congress, whose powers are not touched by it. Look still further at the railroad charters, and even admit that they were grants in the nature of a contract; but you cannot deny that the contract must be interpreted with reference to the Constitution of the United States. Learned judges have held that the law of the place where a contract is made not only regulates and governs it, *but constitutes a part of the contract itself.* (Sturgis *vs.* Crowninshield, 4 Wheat. 122.) But if the law constitutes a part of the contract, still more must the Constitution. Apply this principle and the case is clear. Every railroad charter has been framed subject to the exercise of the acknowledged powers of Congress, all of which are implied in the grant as essential conditions, not less than if they were set forth expressly. The Supreme Court has decided that "all contracts are made subject to the right of *eminent domain*, so that they cannot be considered as violated by the exercise of this right." (The West River Bridge *vs.* Dix, 6 Howard, 507.) But the powers of Congress, invoked on the present occasion to regulate commerce among the several States, to establish post roads, and to raise and equip armies, are in the nature of an *eminent domain*, to which all local charters are subject. Therefore, I repeat again, nothing is proposed "impairing the obligation of a contract," even if that well-known prohibition were applicable to Congress.

From these details of criticism the Senator jumped to a broader proposition. He asserted that the pending measure was destructive of the sovereignty of the States, and he even went so far as to say that it was the same as if you said that all State legislation is null and void. These, sir, were his exact words. How the Senator, even in any ardor of advocacy, could have ventured on this assumption, it is difficult to comprehend. Here is a measure, which, as I have already demonstrated, is founded on three different texts of the Constitution, which is upheld by three unassailable supports, and which is in essential harmony with the Union itself; and yet we are told that it is destructive of the sovereignty of the States. Such an assumption seems uttered in the very wildness of unhesitating advocacy. If it is anything but a phrase, it must be condemned, not only as without foundation, but as hostile to the best interests of the country.

Sir, the pending measure is in no respect destructive of the sovereignty of the States; nor does it in any sense say that all State legislation is null and void. On the contrary, it simply asserts a plain and unquestionable power under the Constitution of the United States. If in any way it seems to touch what is invoked as State sovereignty, or to set aside any State legislation, it is only in pursuance of the Constitution. It is simply because the Constitution, and the laws made in pursuance thereof, are *the supreme law of the land.*

But the assumptions of the Senator bring me back to the vital principle with which I began. After exhibiting the public convenience involved in the present question, I said that it concerned still more the unity of the Republic. It is in short that identical question, which has so often entered this Chamber, and which is now convulsing this land with bloody war. It is the question of the Union itself. In his ardor for that vampire monopoly which, brooding over New Jersey, sucks the life-blood of the whole country, the Senator from Maryland sets up most dangerous pretensions in the name of State rights. Sir, the Senator flings into one scale the pretensions of State rights. Into the other scale I fling the Union itself.

Sir, the Senator from Maryland is a practiced lawyer, and he cannot have forgotten that Nathan Dane, whose name is an authority in our courts, tells us plainly that the terms "sovereign States," "State sovereignty," "State rights," and "rights of States," are not constitutional expressions." Others of equal weight in the early history of the country have said the same thing. Mr. Madison, in the Convention which framed the Constitution, said, "Some contend that States are *sovereign*, when, in fact, they are only political societies. The States never possessed the essential right of sovereignty. These were always vested in Congress." Elbridge Gerry of Massachusetts, in the same Convention, said: "It appears to me that the States never were independent. They had only corporate rights." General Pinckney, of South Carolina, said: "I hold it for a fundamental point, that an individual independence of the States is utterly irreconcilable with the idea of an aggregate sovereignty." (Madison Papers, page 631.) Both Patrick Henry and George Mason, in the Virginia convention, opposed the Constitution on the very ground that it superseded State Rights. But, perhaps, the true intention of the authors of the Constitution may be best found in the letter of General Washington, as President of the Convention, transmitting it to congress. Here are his words:

"It is obviously impracticable *in the Federal Government of these States to secure all rights of independent sovereignty to each*, and yet provide for the safety of all. Individuals entering into society must give up a share of liberty to preserve the rest." * * * * "In all our deliberations we kept steadily in view that which appears to us the greatest interest of every true American—*the consolidation of our Union*—in which is involved our prosperity, safety, perhaps our national existence.

"GEORGE WASHINGTON."

I content myself on this head when I find myself with the support of this great name.

By the adoption of the Constitution the people of the United States constituted themselves *a nation*, one and indivisible, with all the unity and power of a nation. They were no longer a confederation, subject to the disturbing pretensions, prejudices, and whims of its component parts, but they became a body-politic, where every part was subordinate to the Constitution, as every part of the natural body is subordinate to the principle of life. The sovereignty of the United States, where all are but "parts of one stupendous whole." The powers then and there conferred upon the nation were supreme. And it is those very powers which I now invoke, in the name of the Union, and to the end that pretensions in the name of State rights may be overthrown.

I have already presented a picture of these intolerable pretensions. But they must be examined more minutely. They may be seen, *first*, in their character as a monopoly; and, *secondly*, in their character as a Usurpation under the Constitution of the United States. I need not say that in each they are equally indefensible.

If you go back to the earliest days of English history, you will find that monopolies have from the beginning been odious, as contrary to the ancient and fundamental laws of the realm. A writer, who is often quoted in the courts, says: "Monopolies by common law are void, as being against the freedom of trade and discouraging labor and industry, and putting it in the power of particular persons to set what prices they please on a commodity." (Hawkins's Pleas of Crown, vol. 1, p.—.) But without claiming that the present monopoly is void at common law, it is enough to show its inconsistency with the Constitution. And here I borrow Mr. Webster's language in his famous argument against the monopoly of steam navigation granted by the State of New York, as follows:

"Now I think it very reasonable to say that *the Constitution never intended to leave with the States the power of granting* monopolies either of trade or of navigation; and therefore, that as to this, the commercial power is exclusively in Congress."

Then again he says:

"I insist that the nature of the case and of the power did imperatively require that such important authority as that of granting monopolies of trade and navigation *should not be considered as still retained by the States*."

And then again, he adduces an authority which ought to be conclusive on the present occasion. It is that of New Jersey at an earlier day:

"The New Jersey resolutions (on forming the Constitution of the Udited States,) complain that the regulation of trade was within the power the several States, within their separate jurisdiction, to such a degree as to involve many difficulties and embarrassments; and they express an earnest opinion that *the sole and exclusive power of regulating trade ought to be with Congress*."

And yet, in the face of these principles we have a gigantic monopoly organized by New Jersey, composed of several confederate corporations, whose capital massed together is said to amount to more than $27,537,977—a capital not much inferior to that of the United States Bank, which once seemed to hold "divided empire" with the national Government itself. *Divisum imperium cum Jove Cæsar habet.* And this transcendent monopoly, thus vast in resources, undertakes to levy a toll on the commerce, the passengers, the mails, and the troops of the Union in their transit between two great cities, both of which are outside of New Jersey. In its attitude and in its pretension the grasping monopoly is not unlike Apollyon in Bunyan's Pilgrim's Progress, whose usurpation is thus described:

"But now in this Valley of Humiliation poor Christian was hard put to it; for he had gone but a little way before he espied a foul fiend coming over the field to meet him; his name was Apollyon. Then did Christian begin to be afraid, and to cast in his mind whether to go back or to stand his ground." * * * *

"Now, the monster was hideous to behold; he was clothed with scales like a fish, and they are his pride; he had wings like a dragon, feet like a bear, and out of his belly came fire and smoke, and his mouth was as the mouth of a lion. When he was come up to Christian, he beheld him with a disdainful countenance, and thus began to question him:

"APOLLYON. Whence come you, and whither are you bound?

"CHRISTIAN. I am come from the city of Destruction, which is the place of all evil, and am going to the city of Zion.

"APOLLYON. By this I perceive that thou art one of my subjects; for all that country is mine, and I am the prince and god of i.."

New Jersey is the Valley of Humiliation trhough which all travelers north and south from the city of New York to the city of Washington must pass; and the monopoly, like Apollyon, claims them all as "subjects," saying, "for all that country is mine, and I am the prince and god of it."

The enormity of this Usurpation may be seen in its natural consequences. New Jersey claims the right to levy a tax for State revenue on passengers and freight in transit across her territory from State to State; in other words, to levy a tax on "commerce among the several States." *Of course the right to tax is the right to prohibit.* The same power which can exact "ten cents from every passenger" according to the cry of the Camden and Amboy Railroad, by the voice of its counsel, may exact ten dollars or any other sum, and thus effectively close this great avenue of communication.

But if New Jersey can successfully play this game of taxation, and compel tribute from the domestic commerce of the Union as it traverses her territory on the way from State to State, then may every other State do likewise. New York, with her central power, may build up an overshadowing monopoly and a boundless revenue, while all the products and population of the West traversing her territory on their way to the sea, and all the products and population of the East, with the contributions of foreign commerce, traversing her territory on their way to the West, are compelled to pay tribute. Pennsylvania, holding one of the great highways of the Union; Maryland, constituting an essential link in the chain of communication with the national capital; Ohio, spanning from lake to river, and forming a mighty ligament of States, East and West; Indiana, enjoying the same unsurpassed opportunities; Illinois, girdled by States with all of which it is dove-tailed by railroads east and west, north and south; Kentucky, guarding the gates of the Southwest; and finally, any one of the States on the long line of the Pacific railroad may enter upon a similar career of unscrupulous exaction until anarchy sits supreme, and there are as many different tributes as there are States. If the Union should continue to exist, it would be only as a name. The national unity would be destroyed.

The taste of revenue is to a Government like the taste of blood to a wild beast, quickening and maddening the energies, so that it becomes too deaf to all suggestions of injustice; and the difficulties must increase where this taxation is enforced by a far reaching monopoly. The State once tasting this blood, sees only an easy way of obtaining the means it desires; and other States will yield to the same temptation. The poet, after picturing vice as a monster of frightful mien, tells us in familiar words—

"Yet seen too oft, familiar with her face,
We first endure, then pity, then embrace."

A profitable Usurpation, like that of New Jersey, would be a tempting example to other States. "It is only the first step which costs." Let this Usurpation be sanctioned by Congress, and you hand over the domestic commerce of the Union to a succession of local imposts. Each State will be a tax gatherer at the expense of the Union. Each State will play the part of Don Quixotte, and the Union will be Sancho Panza, bound not only to contributions, but also compelled to receive on the bare back the lashes which were the penance of the knightly adventurer. If there be any single fruit of our national unity, if there be any single element of the Union. if there be any single triumph of the Constitution which may be placed above all others, it is the freedom of commerce between the States, under which that *free trade*, which is the aspiration of philosophers, is assured to all citizens of the Union, as they circulate through our whole broad country, without hindrance from any State. But this vital principle is now in jeopardy.

Do not forget that it is the tax imposed on commerce between New York and Philadelphia, two cities outside of the State of New Jersey, which I denounce. I have denounced it as hostile to the Union. I also denounce it as hostile to the spirit of the age, which is everywhere overturning the barriers of commerce. The robber castles, which once compelled the payment of toll on the Rhine, were long ago dismantled, and exist now only as monuments of picturesque beauty. Kindred pretensions in other places have been overthrown or trampled out. The duties levied by Denmark on all vessels passing through the Sound and the Belts, the duties levied by Hanover on the goods of all nations at Stade on the Elbe; the tolls exacted on the Danube in its protracted course; the tolls exacted by Holland on the busy waters of the Scheldt, and all transit imposts within the great Zoll-Verein of Germany have all been abolished; and in this work of enfranchisement the Government of the United States led the way, insisting, in the words of President Pierce, in his annual message, "on the right of *free transit* into and from the Baltic." But the right of free transit across the States of the Union is now assailed. Strange that you should reach so far to secure *free transit* in the Baltic and should hesitate in its defense here at home!

Thank God! within the bounds of the Union, under the national Constitution, commerce is free. As the *open sea* is the highway of nations, so is this Union the highway of the States, with all their commerce, and no State can claim any exclusive property therein. The Union is a *mare librum* beyond the power of any State, and not a *mare clausum*, subject to as many tyrannies as there are States. And yet the State of New Jersey now asserts the power of closing a highway of the Union.

Such a pretension, so irrational and destructive, cannot be dealt with tenderly. Like the serpent, it must be bruised on the head. Nor can there be any delay. Every moment of life yielded to such a Usurpation is like the concession once in an evil hour yielded to nullification, which was kindred in origin and character, The present pretension of New Jersey belongs to the same school with that abhorred and blood-bespattered pretension of South Carolina.

Perhaps, sir, it is not unnatural that the doctrines of South Carolina on State rights should obtain a shelter in New Jersey. Like seeks like. There is a common bond among the sciences, among the virtues, among the vices, and so, also, among the monopolies. The monopoly which was founded on the hideous pretension of property in man obtained a responsive sympathy in that other monopoly which was founded on the greed of unjust taxation, and both were naturally upheld in the name of State rights. Both must be overthrown in the name of the Union. South Carolina must cease to be a slave State, and so must New Jersey. All hail to the genius of universal emancipation! All hail to the Union, victorious over the Rebellion, victorious also over a Usurpation which menaces the unity of the Republic!

www.ingramcontent.com/pod-product-compliance
Lightning Source LLC
LaVergne TN
LVHW020641110826
845149LV00004B/1314

9781418189556